Playing

Written and illustrated
by Tim Hopgood

Collins

I like playing.

2

We like playing.

5

We like playing in the rain.

We like playing in the wind.

We like playing in the snow.

We like playing in the mud.

A story map

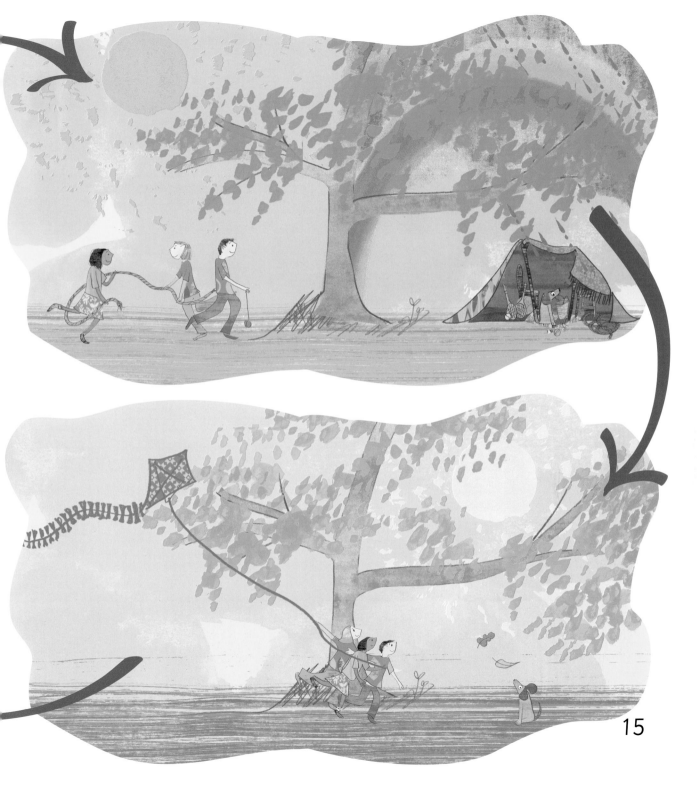

✿ Ideas for guided reading ✿

Learning objectives: use language to imagine and recreate roles and experiences; read a range of familiar and common words and simple sentences independently; retell narratives in the correct sequence, drawing on the language patterns of stories

Curriculum links: Knowledge and Understanding of the World: Find out about their environment, and talk about the features they like and dislike

High frequency words: I, like, we, in, the

Interest words: playing, rain, wind, snow, mud

Word count: 30

Resources: season cards for spring, summer, autumn and winter

Getting started

- Ask children to take turns to describe what outdoor games they like playing best. Question the children about where they play the games.

- Look at the front and back covers together. In pairs, ask children to read the title and blurb. Invite a volunteer to read the blurb to the group.

- Ask children to suggest what other types of weather they like to play in.

Reading and responding

- Read pp2–3 together. Ask children to look closely at the pictures to describe what is happening to a partner.

- Question the children to develop their understanding, e.g. *What is the weather like? What is the child playing? What has she got with her? What season is it?*

- Ask children to read pp4–13, finding out as much as they can from each page.

- Remind children to use the pictures and meaning to help them read unfamiliar words.